INVESTIGATING SCIENCE CHALLENGES

Investigating FORCES AND MOTION

Richard Spilsbury

CRABTREE
PUBLISHING COMPANY
WWW.CRABTREEBOOKS.COM

CRABTREE
PUBLISHING COMPANY
WWW.CRABTREEBOOKS.COM

Author: Richard Spilsbury

Editors: Sarah Eason, Jennifer Sanderson,
  Petrice Custance, Reagan Miller

Proofreaders: Kris Hirschmann, Janine Deschenes

Indexer: Harriet McGregor

Editorial director: Kathy Middleton

Design: Emma DeBanks

Cover design and additional artwork: Emma DeBanks

Photo research: Rachel Blount

**Production coordinator and
  prepress technician:** Tammy McGarr

Print coordinator: Katherine Berti

Consultant: David Hawksett

Produced for Crabtree Publishing Company by Calcium Creative

Photo Credits:

t=Top, tr=Top Right, tl=Top Left

Inside: Shutterstock: Action Sports Photography: p. 7c; Aspen Photo: p. 4; Cyo Bo: pp. 26-27; BUGNUT23: p. 12b; Dima Fadeev: p. 5; Homydesign: pp. 14-15; lzf: pp. 6-7; Kokhanchikov: p. 22; David Litman: pp. 1; MAGC63: pp. 12-13t; Oneinchpunch: p. 9c; Luca Santilli: p. 19; Shcherbinator: p. 21; Ljupco Smokovski: pp. 8-9; Valenta: p. 15t; Wavebreakmedia: pp. 18, 23; Wikimedia Commons: NASA; edited by Jjron: p. 20.

Cover: Tudor Photography.

Library and Archives Canada Cataloguing in Publication

Spilsbury, Richard, 1963-, author
    Investigating forces and motion / Richard Spilsbury.

(Investigating science challenges)
Includes index.
Issued in print and electronic formats.
ISBN 978-0-7787-4205-0 (hardcover).--
ISBN 978-0-7787-4253-1 (softcover).--
ISBN 978-1-4271-2009-0 (HTML)

    1. Force and energy--Juvenile literature. 2. Motion--Juvenile literature. 3. Physics--Juvenile literature. I. Title.

QC73.4.S662 2018   j531'.6   C2017-907736-8
                                           C2017-907737-6

Library of Congress Cataloging-in-Publication Data

Names: Spilsbury, Richard, 1963- author.
Title: Investigating forces and motion / Richard Spilsbury.
Description: New York, New York : Crabtree Publishing, [2018] |
Series: Investigating science challenges | Audience: Ages 8-11. |
    Audience: Grades 4 to 6. | Includes index.
Identifiers: LCCN 2017057532 (print) | LCCN 2017059304 (ebook) |
    ISBN 9781427120090 (Electronic HTML) |
    ISBN 9780778742050 (reinforced library binding : alk. paper) |
    ISBN 9780778742531 (pbk. : alk. paper)
Subjects: LCSH: Force and energy--Juvenile literature. | Motion--
    Juvenile literature. | Physics--Juvenile literature.
Classification: LCC QC73.4 (ebook) | LCC QC73.4 .S66225 2018 (print)
    | DDC 531.6--dc23
LC record available at https://lccn.loc.gov/2017057532

Crabtree Publishing Company
www.crabtreebooks.com   1-800-387-7650

Printed in the U.S.A./022018/CG20171220

Published in Canada
Crabtree Publishing
616 Welland Ave.
St. Catharines, Ontario
L2M 5V6

Published in the United States
Crabtree Publishing
PMB 59051
350 Fifth Avenue, 59th Floor
New York, New York 10118

Published in the United Kingdom
Crabtree Publishing
Maritime House
Basin Road North, Hove
BN41 1WR

Published in Australia
Crabtree Publishing
3 Charles Street
Coburg North
VIC, 3058

CONTENTS

FORCES MAKE THINGS MOVE

From bicycles racing and balls bouncing, to dogs running and people dancing, there are many different kinds of motion. Motion is a change of position or location, such as the way an arm moves up and down or how a train travels from one place to another. Motion is important to our lives and affects the things that we do every day. Nothing moves by itself. Any kind of motion requires a **force** to cause the change.

Basketball players apply a force to the ball as they push down on the ball to bounce it.

downward motion

A sailboard moves forward when wind creates a pushing force against its wide, open sails.

forward motion

Forces in Action

Things that are stationary stay still until a force makes them move. Forces cause and create motion. A force is a push or a pull on an object. Things move only when they are pushed or pulled in some way. When you push on a door or pull on a drawer handle, you are applying a force to those things. This force makes things move. It makes them change their motion. There are many different kinds of forces that can make things move. Wind is moving air and it can blow a kite to make it move. The rush of moving water in a river can push against a raft to change its motion or location.

INVESTIGATE

Scientists **observe** the world around them and ask questions. They then plan and carry out **investigations** to find answers. In this book, you will carry out investigations to answer questions about forces and motion. On pages 28 and 29 you can find investigation tips, check your work, and read suggestions for other investigations you can try.

SLOWING DOWN

If you kick a ball along the ground, why does it not stay in motion and keep moving forever? Why does it eventually stop? A moving object will continue at a steady speed if no forces are acting upon it. The ball slows down because while the force of your kick started its motion, another force worked to slow down and eventually stop that motion. A force is needed to cause any change in motion. The force that **resists** motion is called **friction**. Friction always works to stop things from moving, or to slow them down when they are moving. The less friction there is, the longer objects in motion can keep moving.

Friction and **air resistance** will slow down a skateboard, so you have to keep pushing your feet against the ground to keep moving forward.

Friction in Action

The force of friction is caused by two surfaces that come into contact with each other, such as a ball rolling across the ground. Even if the ball and the ground look fairly smooth, up close you would see a lot of little bumps and pits, which make their surfaces snag together and cause friction. Friction does not only exist between two solid surfaces. For example, when a boat is on water, the water rubbing against the bottom of the boat slows it down. This friction is called **water resistance**. The friction between a moving object and air is called air resistance.

Race cars may use a parachute to increase air resistance and help them stop.

Useful Friction

Friction can be annoying because it slows us down when we want to keep going, but it is useful when we want to stop. The brakes on a bicycle use friction to stop wheels from turning and bicycles from moving. When you squeeze the brake handle, this makes brake pads push against the wheels to make them stop.

FEEL THE FORCE!

When you push down on the pedals of a bicycle, the force of your legs moves the wheels and makes the bicycle move forward. As you go forward, the air you are moving through is pushing back against you and slowing you down. The surface of the tires rubbing against the surface of the road also creates friction that tries to slow you down.

Professional cyclists use very thin, smooth tires, called slicks, to minimize friction and help them move as fast as possible.

How Strong is the Force?

The strength of the force of friction depends on the surfaces rubbing together. If the surfaces are smooth, there will be less friction than if the surfaces are rough. For example, people slide a long way on ice because the ice is extremely smooth and there is little friction. Friction also produces heat. On a cold day, you rub your hands together to keep warm. It is the force of friction between the surfaces of your hands that makes them warm up.

Get a Grip!

The soles of your shoes grip the ground as you walk. Friction causes this grip, whether you are walking on a sidewalk, sand, grass, or gravel. On a very smooth surface, such as ice, there is less friction and the soles of your shoes may not have enough grip to keep you from falling over.

Hikers wear boots with good grip to create friction between their boots and the ground.

INVESTIGATE

You can see friction at work if you walk on a smooth surface wearing different kinds of footwear. How much friction would you experience if you walked on a smooth surface while wearing shoes with good grip, such as sneakers? How might it be different if you walked on a smooth surface wearing only socks? Which footwear would create more friction? Which would be easier to walk in? Why?

9

Let's Investigate

SCIENCE FRICTION

Friction is a force that affects the speed at which something moves. Do you notice how the speed at which you move changes when you ride a bike or a skateboard over different surfaces? This is caused by rolling friction. Let's investigate how different surfaces affect rolling friction.

You Will Need:

- A skateboard
- Access to two different surfaces. One must be a smooth surface, such as a concrete playground. The second surface can be of your choosing (follow the instructions opposite step 4).
- A friend
- A stopwatch
- A pen
- A sheet of paper

Step 1: Put your skateboard on a smooth surface, such as concrete. Get ready to push yourself forward.

Step 2: Ask your friend to start timing with the stopwatch as soon as you push yourself forward.

Step 3: Push yourself forward and let your friend time how long it takes for your skateboard to come to a stop as it rolls across the surface. Write down the time.

Science Challenge

Step 4: Now you will need to repeat the experiment. However, this time you will need to choose a surface that you think will make your time slower than on the smooth surface. Remember what you have already learned in this book about rolling friction. What type of surface do you think will slow your skateboard?

Challenge Questions

- What second surface did you choose to travel on and why?
- What was the difference in time between your experiment in step 1 and your experiment in step 4?
- Why is it important to push yourself forward on the skateboard with the same force each time?

SPEEDING UP

A powerful motorcycle can go much faster than a bicycle. A jet plane can go faster than a paper plane. The reason is that both the motorcycle and the jet plane have powerful **engines** that can produce larger forces than the legs of a rider or the arm of the person throwing the paper plane. Larger pushes or pulls cause greater changes in motion in any object. Kicking a ball hard makes it go farther than kicking it softly.

Distance and Time

Speed is a measure of the distance traveled in a particular amount of time. If a person on a bicycle travels 50 miles (80 km) in one hour, we say his or her speed was 50 miles per hour (80 km/h). A car speeding along at 100 miles per hour (161 km/h) covers twice the distance in the same amount of time. At this speed we can predict that in 30 minutes, or half an hour, the car will have traveled 50 miles (80 km), or half the distance it would travel in an hour.

The world's top sprinters can run the 100-meter race in just over 9.5 seconds. This is an average speed of just over 23 miles per hour (37 km/h).

A cheetah can use the force of its leg muscles to **accelerate** from a standstill to a speed of 60 miles per hour (96 km/h) in just four seconds!

Changing Speed

The speed of an object during a trip is often an average speed. That is because things do not always move at the same speed at every point of the trip. For example, the bike is stationary at the start of its trip, so its speed is zero. Then the rider pushes hard and fast on the pedals to speed up, or accelerate. The rider may go faster than 50 miles per hour (80 km/h) for part of the trip, if there is an extra push from the wind behind him or her. The rider may go slower for other parts, perhaps because there is a slower rider or an obstacle in front of him or her. Then he or she will have to slow down, or **decelerate**.

13

CHANGING DIRECTION

Forces such as friction can slow the speed of a moving object, but they can also change its direction of motion. When we use a force to put an object into motion, such as hitting a tennis ball over the net, it moves in the direction of the force we apply. When our opponent hits the ball back, the new force will make the ball return in a different direction.

Turning

If one bumper car bashes into the left side of a second bumper car that is moving forward, the force will make the second car change direction to the right. A bumper car will also change direction when a driver steers it. Turning left, the wheels twist left, too. Then the friction force on the left-hand wheels is greater than that on the right-hand wheels. The right-hand wheels turn faster and push the bumper car to the left. A ship with a **propeller** moves straight forward by pushing water backward past a flat, vertical blade called a **rudder**. Twisting the rudder to the right makes the water push against its right side. This force makes the rear of the ship move sideways to the left, so the front of the ship turns right.

Propellers spin to push water backward. This causes the surrounding sea to push a ship forward. When a rudder catches some of the propeller's force, it changes the ship's direction.

rudder

propeller

Snowboarders change direction by tilting their snowboard to push down into the snow on one side. This increases friction between that edge and the snow. Then that edge moves slower than the other, so the board twists to face in a different direction.

INVESTIGATE

Sailboats at sea wanting to go in a particular direction have a problem when the wind changes where it is blowing from. Suddenly the wind is no longer pushing the boat from behind, but instead from the side. What do sailors do to the sails to catch the wind's force and continue moving forward?

15

SET SAIL!

Vehicles can change their direction by changing the angle of parts such as wheels or rudders. When the direction of a force from the side varies, some vehicles can move parts to make sure they continue moving in their chosen direction. Let's investigate how forces affect direction.

You Will Need:
- An empty small juice box with its straw
- Clear tape
- A pair of scissors
- Cardboard
- A jug of water
- A shallow tray
- A compass
- A bicycle pump
- An adult to help

Step 1: Remove the straw from the top of the juice box and tape the hole closed. Ask an adult to use the scissors to pierce a new hole just big enough for the straw in the center of the front of the box.

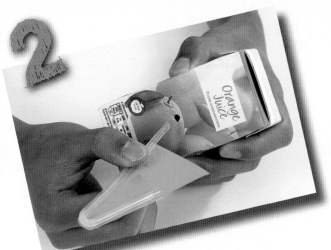

Step 2: Make a sail by cutting a triangle of cardboard to fit between the long part of the straw (the mast) and the shorter piece that folds over. Tape the cardboard in place. Insert the mast into the hole you made in step 1.

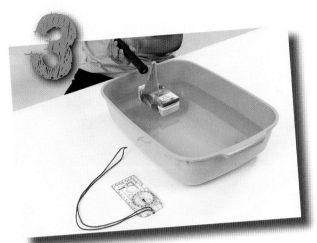

Step 3: Pour water into your tray until it is half full. Then put the compass next to the tray and twist the tray so its long side is pointing north. Float the boat on the water near one short end and turn the sail so it is pointing east. Now use the pump to blow air at the sail from behind the carton. In which direction does the carton move?

Step 4: Now repeat the experiment, but this time blow the air from the southeast. Can you predict which direction you will have to turn the sail so the boat travels forward? What will happen to the boat if you blow from different directions, but do not change the angle of the sail?

Science Challenge

Challenge Questions

- What sail direction did you choose to ensure the boat moved forward. Explain your thinking.
- Did the boat always move forward if you changed the direction from which you blew air?
- When the air is blowing straight ahead, which sail direction do you think would be the least effective in moving the boat forward?
- Why is it important to produce the same force of air through the pump?

BALANCED AND UNBALANCED

The reason an object stays still, moves, speeds up, slows down, or changes direction is explained by whether the forces acting on it are **balanced** or **unbalanced**. When two equal-sized forces push in opposite directions, they cancel each other out. They are balanced. If you and a friend both push with equal force on a door from opposite sides, the door should stay still. The forces you both used balanced or canceled each other out, so neither of you managed to move the door. Things move, speed up, slow down, or change direction when forces are unbalanced.

When opposite forces are balanced, which means that the two teams pictured above pull with equal strength, they will not move. If one side pulls with more strength, the forces are unbalanced and that team can pull the opposing team toward it, winning the tug-of-war game.

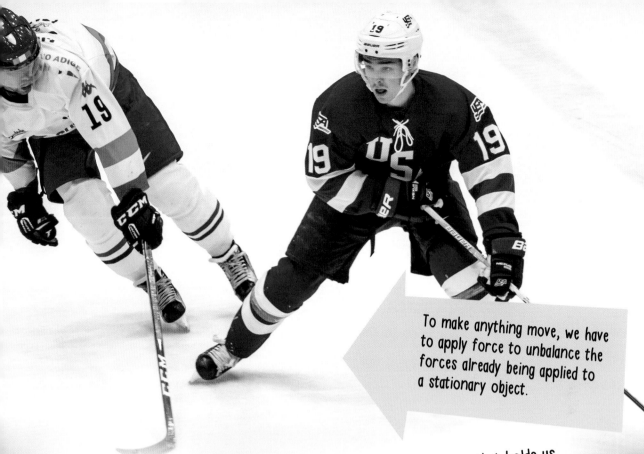

To make anything move, we have to apply force to unbalance the forces already being applied to a stationary object.

A Balancing Act

Gravity is an invisible force that pulls things down. It is the force that holds us to Earth's surface. Earth's gravity pulls objects toward the center of the planet. So when you drop a ball, it falls to the ground instead of floating away. When we rest a book on a table, the force of gravity is pulling it down and the upward **normal force** exerted by the table is pushing it up by an equal amount of force. You can feel this force yourself if you try pushing down on a table. The forces are balanced, so the book stays still on the table.

Changing Motions

When forces are different in size, they are unbalanced and do not cancel each other out. Imagine that two forces are acting at the same time on an object that is moving straight ahead. One is a very strong force toward the left, and the other is a weaker force toward the right. Since the force toward the left is stronger, the object changes direction and starts moving to the left. Tilting a table unbalances the forces on a book resting on it. With a steeper tilt, the normal force on the book becomes less than gravity, and eventually the pull down the slope will be greater than friction, so the book slides and falls.

19

GOING UP AND DOWN

Gravity has a huge impact on the way things move. It makes all things fall to the ground when they are not supported by something pushing upward with an equal force. When you are riding a bicycle, gravity speeds you up as you travel down a hill. As you go uphill, gravity tries to pull you down, so you have to push against the pedals with more force to fight against gravity.

Flying High

Spacecraft engines have to be incredibly powerful to provide enough force to unbalance the force of gravity that tries to hold a rocket on Earth. The engines also have to fight against the friction or air resistance that pushes against it. If you let the air out of a balloon, the air goes one way and the balloon moves in the opposite direction. Rockets work in a similar way. Rocket engines burn **fuel** to produce **gases** that shoot out of the engine **nozzle** at high speed. As these gases push down, they push the rocket upward. A rocket has to reach a speed of 17,400 miles per hour (28,000 km/h) to be moving fast enough to escape Earth's gravity in order to travel beyond Earth's **atmosphere** into space.

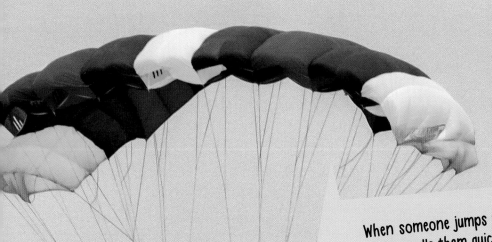

When someone jumps from an aircraft, gravity pulls them quickly toward the ground. When they open the parachute, the parachute causes a lot of air resistance. This force works in an opposite direction to gravity and slows them down so they can land safely.

Dropping Down

When a spacecraft returns to Earth, gravity helps it come down again, just as it makes everything else fall to Earth. The problem is that gravity can pull things down very fast. The friction created by air resistance is not strong enough to stop objects from falling, but it can stop them from speeding up. People can increase air resistance to stay in the air for longer. When a spacecraft lands or people jump from an airplane, they use a parachute to make them fall more gently.

The rockets carrying the heavy space shuttle toward space from the ground produce as much push as around 37,000 Formula One car engines!

PATTERNS OF MOTION

Every day, and usually without even thinking about it, we anticipate the effects of forces on an object's motion. That is because the combination of balanced and unbalanced forces acting on an object can be used to predict and describe its movement. For example, we know that when we throw something up in the air, it will fall down again. We know that when we are playing jump rope, the rope moves in a repetitive pattern, forward and backward. That is how we know when it is time for us to jump without becoming tangled.

A grandfather clock has a large pendulum swinging in a repetitive back-and-forth motion.

Swinging Up and Down

There are many more examples of repetitive motion or patterns of motion. Most of these are when the object in motion is moving from or around a fixed location. Think of a car's windshield wipers or a pendulum in a grandfather clock. A pendulum is an object or weight hung from a fixed point on a rope or rod, which swings freely back and forth because of gravity. A swing is a kind of pendulum. When you lift a swing back and let it go, it moves because of the force of gravity. When it swings up the other way, gravity moves it back again. Pendulums keep moving backward and forward, or side to side, until air resistance slows and stops them.

When we create a regular pattern of motion with a loop of rope, we can jump over it at its lowest point.

In Orbit

Earth, like other nearby planets including Jupiter and Mars, moves in a loop around the Sun called an **orbit**. The Sun is so huge that it has a very powerful gravity, so it pulls the planets toward it. At the same time as the planets fall toward the Sun, they are also moving sideways around the Sun. Imagine swinging a ball around on the end of a rope. The ball is being pulled toward you, but its sideways motion keeps it going around. Although the Sun's gravity pulls on the planets, the planets have enough sideways motion to keep them going around in their orbits.

INVESTIGATE

Imagine you are at the park, sitting on a swing. What will happen when you give yourself a push with your feet? What do you predict your pattern of motion will be on the swing? Which direction will you swing? Now think about the difference between a toddler's swing and a swing for an older child. Why do you think the older child's swing has longer ropes or chains? Which swing will go higher?

IN THE SWING

The time it takes for a pendulum to go backward and forward or a person on a swing in a park to be pushed and then return for another push is called a **period**. How do you think the period of a pendulum or swing is related to the length of its string? Will a longer pendulum have a longer period than a shorter one? Let's investigate how gravity affects the period of a pendulum.

You Will Need:

- Small, medium, and large weights such as washer rings, stones, or small, heavy balls
- A ruler, yardstick, or meterstick
- A table
- Heavy books
- Three pieces of string of different lengths: 8, 20, 31 inches (20, 50, 80 cm)
- A friend
- A stopwatch
- A notebook
- A pen

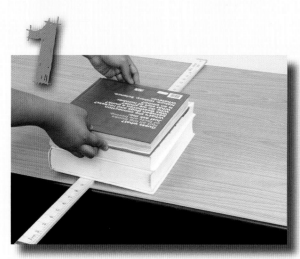

Step 1: Place your ruler, meterstick, or yardstick so it hangs off the edge of the table. Weigh it down with some heavy books so it does not move.

Step 2: Tie the medium weight to one end of the 20-inch (50-cm) string. Tie the other end to the ruler.

Step 3: Pull back the weight so the string is in line with the table edge. The string should be stretched so it is straight and horizontal. To make the test fair, countdown from three so that your friend starts timing with the stopwatch at the exact same time as you let go. Your friend must stop the stopwatch as soon as the pendulum returns to its original position after one period. Release the pendulum. Write down the result. Repeat three times, then add up the times and divide by three to get an average time.

Step 4: Now repeat this experiment, but this time choose the string that you think will have a longer period than the one used in steps 1 to 3. Using what you have learned about gravity and patterns of motion, why do you think you need to make sure you always pull the weight back the same distance each time? What do you predict will happen?

- Was there a difference in the average time each pendulum completed one period? If so, which string had the longest and which the shortest period?
- Try changing the weight and the height at which you release the pendulum. Does the period change with the size of the weight you put on the pendulum or the height at which you released the pendulum? If it did change, why do you think that was so?

INVESTIGATE MORE

All the movements we see around us, from a flying bird to the moving second hand on a clock face, are produced and controlled by forces. Objects that are sitting still do not move because different forces acting on them cancel each other out. Once a force causes an to object move, the object will keep moving in the same direction unless another force slows it down or forces the object to change direction.

World of Forces

Forces are not only the result of pushes and pulls from engines, pedals, living things, gravity, and friction. If you have ever been on a trampoline, you were relying on **tension force** and **spring force** to have fun. Try doing some of your own research. How are tension and spring forces different? Why is the pull of gravity on an object in space different from its pull on you at Earth's surface? **Magnetism** and **static electricity** are other invisible natural forces like gravity. What causes these forces?

Maglev is short for magnetic levitation. Because of magnetism, maglev trains levitate, or hover, above the tracks to help them go fast.

Changing the Balance

The major force slowing most heavy trains down is friction. Scientists invented the maglev train to completely change the balance between the forward push of the engine and the backward force of friction, in order to go faster. This system uses the push of powerful magnets against each other to lift a train off its tracks as it moves along. Maglev trains are the fastest on Earth at speeds of 375 miles per hour (604 km/h), yet they can use less energy to move forward than similar-sized normal trains. What other ways do people reduce friction to change the balance of forces and improve the energy efficiency of machines? To start, you could research the following topics: bulbous bows, Teflon, and spoilers.

INVESTIGATE

Streamlining is a way of reducing the friction that works to slow down objects that are moving. For example, rockets and aircraft are streamlined machines that have smooth sides to slip past the air and their shape reduces air resistance. Many animals are streamlined. Investigate the different body shapes and outer surfaces of dolphins, penguins, and sand swimmers. Why is being streamlined helpful to them? Now investigate the body shapes and behaviors that increase resistance in jellyfish and flying squirrels. How is this helpful to them?

Science Challenge
TIPS

Pages 10-11: Science Friction

To move slower, you should choose a surface that is rougher. These surfaces create more friction with the wheels of the skateboard than the smooth surface. Some of the surfaces you could have chosen include a grassy lawn, a gravel path, wooden decking, a sand pit, and a muddy field.

The time difference depends on how rough the surface is. You should find that the rougher the surface is, the slower your time should be. For example, gloopy mud is probably slower to cross than wooden decking. If there is no time difference, you may have pushed off with more forward force on the rough surface than the smooth surface, or it may be that the smooth surface is pitted and worn, which would slow you down. The investigation is fair and accurate when you push yourself with the same force.

You could also investigate where surfaces that cause friction are used. For example, why do sidewalks have slightly bumpy surfaces? How could this help us when it rains?

Page 16-17: Set Sail!

The boat will probably move forward most easily with the sail twisted to point southwest according to the compass. Then the face of the sail is **perpendicular** to the force of the moving air, so it blows over its whole surface area.

Moving the pump to different positions changes the amount of air hitting the sail if the sail stays in one position. When the air is pushing end-on to the sail, it pushes on just a small surface area, so it does not move the boat by much.

The accuracy and fairness of this experiment depends on trying to produce the same force of air from the pump. If one blast of air is faster than another it may make the boat move farther, regardless of the sail position.

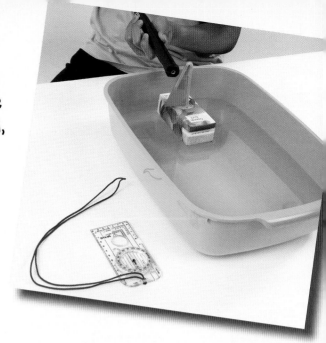

Page 24-25: In the Swing

You should find that the longest string has the longest period and the shortest string has the shortest period. The shortest pendulum can fit more back-and-forth movements in a given time than the longest. We say it has a higher **frequency**.

The weight of the washer ring, stone, or ball should have no effect on the period. This is because the pull of gravity is the same on any mass, however big. The angle of release of the pendulum should also have no effect. Releasing the pendulum allows the pull of gravity to accelerate the weight down to the lowest point, at which time it continues moving to the same height from which it was released, then falls back, and so on. With a higher release point, there is more time for the weight to accelerate, so it moves fast before it reaches the low point. With a lower release point, there is less time for acceleration, so the weight reaches a lower speed. In each case, the period is the same.

GLOSSARY

accelerate Speed up

air resistance The push of air against moving things that can slow them down. Air resistance is a type of friction.

atmosphere The layer of gases around a planet

balanced When there is an even weight or force from both sides

decelerate Slow down

engines Machines with moving parts that convert power into motion

force The effect that causes things to move in a particular way, usually a push or a pull

frequency The number of regular movements in a given amount of time

friction The action of one object or surface moving across another. Friction is a force that can slow things down.

fuel A material such as coal, natural gas, or oil that is burned to produce heat or power

gases Substances that are often invisible, do not keep their shape, or always take up the same amount of space

investigations Procedures carried out to observe, study, or test something in order to learn more about it

maglev A high-speed train that runs on magnets above a magnetic track

magnetism A force that attracts certain metals

normal force The support force exerted upon an object that is in contact with another object

nozzle A spout that directs the flow of water or gas from a pipe

observe To use your senses to gather information

orbit The curved path in space that is followed by an object going around and around a planet, moon, or star

pendulum A hanging weight that swings backward and forward

period The length of time it takes for a pendulum to make one full swing and return to its original position

perpendicular At 90 degrees to something else

propeller A device with blades used for moving a boat or aircraft

resists To withstand an action or effect

rudder A flat, movable piece of wood or metal used to steer a ship, boat, or airplane

spring force The force exerted by a compressed or stretched spring upon any object that is attached to it

static electricity Electricity that collects on the surface of something to give it a positive or negative charge and does not flow as a current

tension force The force that is transmitted through a string, rope, cable, or wire when it is pulled tight by forces acting from opposite ends

unbalanced Describes something with one force bigger or stronger than the other

water resistance Friction between a moving object and the water below or around it

LEARNING MORE

Find out more about forces and motion and their uses.

Books

Ives, Rob. *Fun Experiments With Forces and Motion: Hovercrafts, Rockets, and More* (Amazing Science Experiments). Hungry Tomato, 2017.

Kenney, Karen Latchana. *Forces and Motion Investigations* (Key Questions in Physical Science). Lerner Publishing Group, 2017.

Winterberg, Jenna. *Balanced and Unbalanced Forces* (Science Readers: Content and Literacy). Teacher Created Materials, 2015.

Websites

There is more information about forces and motion at:
www.explainthatstuff.com/motion.html

There is a lot to explore at:
http://studyjams.scholastic.com/studyjams/jams/science/forces-and-motion/force-and-motion.htm

There are facts and a quiz on forces and motion at:
www.ducksters.com/science/laws_of_motion.php

INDEX

About the AUTHOR

Richard Spilsbury has a science degree, and has had a lifelong fascination with science. He has written and co-written many books for young people on a wide variety of topics, from ants to avalanches.